WIDE ANGLE
FRAMING YOUR WORLDVIEW

RICK WARREN   CHARLES COLSON

Prison Fellowship
44180 Riverside Parkway
Landsdowne, VA 20176
www.pfm.org

Purpose Driven® Publishing.
1 Saddleback Parkway
Lake Forest, CA 92630
www.purposedriven.com

ISBN 10: 1-4228-0083-0—ISBN 13: 978-1-4228-0083-6

Printed and bound in the United States of America

Table of CONTENTS

Understanding Your Study Guide

Here is a brief explanation of the features of this study guide.

Looking Ahead / Catching Up: You will open each meeting with an opportunity for everyone to check in with each other about how you are doing with the weekly assignments. Accountability is a key to success in this study!

Key Verse: Each week you will find a key verse or Scripture passage for your group to read together. If someone in the group has a different translation, ask them to read it aloud so the group can get a bigger picture of the meaning of the passage.

Video Lessons: There are three video lesson segments for the group to watch together each week. Take notes in the lesson outlines as you watch the video, and be sure to refer back to these notes during your discussion time.

Discovery Questions: Each video segment is complemented by questions for group discussion. Please don't feel pressured to discuss every single question. The material in this study is meant to be your servant, not your master, so there is no reason to rush through the answers. Give everyone ample opportunity to share their thoughts. If you don't get through all of the discovery questions, that's okay.

Living on Purpose: In his book, *The Purpose Driven Life*, Rick Warren identifies God's five purposes for our lives. They are worship, fellowship, discipleship, ministry, and evangelism. We will focus on one or two of these five purposes in each lesson, and discuss how they relate to the subject of the study. This section is very important, so please be sure to leave time for it.

Prayer Direction: At the end of each session you will find suggestions for your group prayer time. Praying together is one of the greatest privileges of small group life. Please don't take it for granted.

Putting It into Practice: We don't want to be just hearers of the Word. We also need to be doers of the Word (James 1:22). This section of the study explains the assignments we would like you to complete before your next meeting. These assignments are application exercises that will help you put into practice the truths you have discussed in the lesson.

Diving Deeper: The material in this small group study is designed to complement the book, *The Good Life*, by Charles Colson (Tyndale, 2005). Each week, this section will direct you to additional reading from the book for greater understanding of the topic. Discovery questions are provided for each of the assigned chapters.

How to Use this Video Curriculum

Follow these six simple steps for a successful small group meeting:

1. Open your group meeting by using the "Looking Ahead" or "Catching Up" sections of your study guide.

2. Watch the video lesson segments together and take notes in the outlines in this study guide. Each video segment is between fifteen and twenty minutes in length.

3. Each video segment is made up of two components. A two-minute highlight from one of Rick Warren's weekend messages sets up the topic of discussion. That's followed by about ten minutes of conversation between Rick and Chuck Colson on the same topic.

4. At the end of each segment, you'll see a Discovery Question on screen. You'll find the same question printed in your study guide. Stop the DVD at that point and discuss the question with your group. You will also find two or three additional questions to expand your discussion if you want to. Take ten minutes or so to discuss the questions, and then move on to the next video segment.

5. Complete the rest of the discussion materials for each session, including the "Living on Purpose" and "Prayer Direction" sections.

6. Review the "Putting It into Practice" assignments and commit to doing them before your next meeting.

Read the Book!

To maximize the impact of this study, each participant should have a copy of both this study guide and the book, *The Good Life*, by Charles Colson. Reading assignments and in-group review of chapters in the book are a vital part of this learning experience. The book will become a valuable, permanent resource for review and sharing once the course has been completed.

MY WORLDVIEW
MATTERS

Looking Ahead .... (10 Minutes)

- Welcome! Begin your time together by reading and discussing the Group Guidelines on page 124.

- Share with the group what you hope to get out of this study.

- Opening Prayer: Pray that God will help you be open to what he wants to teach you through this series.

Key Verse

Host Tip: Ask for a volunteer to read this verse aloud. If anyone has a different translation, ask him or her to read this as well to expand the group's understanding of the verse.

Do not conform any longer to the pattern of this world, but be transformed by the renewing of your mind. Then you will be able to test and approve what God's will is—his good, pleasing and perfect will.

Romans 12:2 (NIV)

Watch the first segment of the video and take notes in the space below. Discuss the questions at the end of the segment.

Notes:

Summary

A worldview is simply the way we think the world works, and how we fit into it. Everyone has a worldview, though most people are not aware of it. Understanding these worldviews is vitally important, because they shape our thoughts, attitudes, and actions.

- Everyone has a worldview.

- Your worldview is the way you think the world works, and how you fit into it.

- Worldviews answer four questions:

  - Where did I come from?

  - Why is the world such a mess?

  - Is there a solution?

  - What is my purpose?

Discovery Questions

1. What differences do worldviews make? Are these differences important?

....

....

....

....

....

Additional Questions for Expanded Discussion

2. Now, having viewed the first Wide Angle discussion, what is your definition of worldview?

3. Based on your current thinking, how would you answer these four essential worldview questions?

   a. Where did I come from?

   b. Why is the world a mess?

   c. Is there a solution?

   d. What is my purpose?

Watch the second segment of the video and take notes in the space below. Discuss the questions at the end of the segment.

Notes:

Summary

Our worldviews will inevitably be shaped either by the media or by the Bible. Unfortunately, Christians have all too often neglected the command to love God with our minds, not just our hearts. This often is a result of having emphasized feeling over thinking. We need to learn to think biblically and to have the integrity to live out what the Bible teaches, since the Bible alone provides a true, livable worldview.

- We are to love God, not just with our hearts and souls, but also with our minds.

- The biblical worldview integrates all parts of life under God and allows us to live with integrity.

- Worldviews contradict each other and can't all be true; only the biblical worldview gives us a complete and true picture of the world as it really is.

Discovery Questions

1. How do you see those around you compartmentalizing their lives? How do you see yourself doing the same thing?

....

....

....

....

....

....

Additional Questions for Expanded Discussion

2. Besides reading the Bible more, how can we begin to conform our minds to a biblical worldview?

3. Where do you see the conflict of worldviews around you?

4. What does "integrity" mean to you?

Watch the third segment of the video and take notes in the space below. Discuss the questions at the end of the segment.

Notes:

Summary

Worldviews have consequences, and false worldviews can be disastrous. The Bible speaks to all of life, and its teachings compete with false worldviews for our allegiance. Since only the biblical worldview accurately describes reality, we need to implement it to avoid disaster. Moreover, to do that, we need to be good stewards of our minds, learning to think biblically and to apply biblical truth to all areas of life.

- Ideas have consequences: *"For as [a man] thinks in his heart, so is he."* (Proverbs 23:7 NKJV)

- The two great themes of the Bible are salvation and stewardship, which includes stewardship of the mind.

- "There is not a square inch in the whole domain of human existence over which Christ, who is sovereign over all, does not cry: 'Mine!'"

Discovery Questions

1. When we look at the world, in what ways do we cry out "mine," when we should cry out "his"?

....

....

....

....

....

....

Additional Questions for Expanded Discussion

2. How do the biblical worldview and the lordship of Christ play out in your daily life?

3. Chuck Colson makes a statement regarding our "responsibility to care for everything God has created and to see all of life through God's eyes." List ways in which you can adhere to these responsibilities.

Living on Purpose .... (10 Minutes)

Discipleship

Developing a biblical worldview means learning to see all of life through God's eyes. Using your current understanding of Scripture and worldview, take some time as a group to list the different areas of your life (work, family, recreation, etc.) and share some ideas together about how we should be thinking about these areas of life from a biblical perspective.

Work:

_____

_____

Family:

_____

_____

Recreation:

_____

_____

Others:

_____

_____

Prayer Direction ....:........................ (10 Minutes)

As you close the meeting:

- Thank God for giving us the Bible as a guidebook to tell us the way the world really works and how we should live in it.

- Ask God to help you see the world the way he sees it, to show you where you need to change, and to give you the wisdom and courage to do so.

Putting It into Practice

Rick and Chuck told us that Christianity is a worldview, one that should shape the way we think about the world, make decisions, and take action. At the same time, false worldviews are influencing the way we look at the world and the way we live. During this week, pay attention to the variety of messages you are getting about worldviews and the four worldview questions. Using your knowledge of the Bible, think of how you should respond. Come prepared to share your thoughts at our next meeting.

Diving Deeper

Read the following chapters of The Good Life, reflect on the Scripture verses listed, and answer the questions.

Chapter 1: The Unavoidable Question

37Jesus answered, " . . . For this purpose I was born and for this purpose I have come into the world—to bear witness to the truth. Everyone who is of the truth listens to my voice." 38Pilate said to him, "What is truth?" (John 18:37–38 ESV)

1. Think of the people who have influenced your worldview. How do you think those who have influenced your worldview would answer Pilate's question?

   ....

   ....

   ....

2. How do you define truth?

   ....

   ....

   ....

Chapter 2: A Shattered Life

And Samuel said, "Has the Lord *as great delight in burnt offerings and sacrifices, as in obeying the voice of the* Lord*? Behold, to obey is better than sacrifice . . . "* (1 Samuel 15:22 ESV)

Many people give little thought to God, but when problems arise, they suddenly want to go to God for help.

1. When you are in trouble, what are some of the ways you turn to "burnt offerings and sacrifices" to get right with God?

....

....

....

Chapter 3: The Great Paradoxes

"Whoever finds his life will lose it, and whoever loses his life for my sake will find it." (Matthew 10:39 ESV)

"Whoever dies with the most toys wins." —Anonymous

1. Why are we so inclined to seek happiness by gaining things for ourselves?

....

....

....

2. What is your response to Jesus' assertion about "losing" our lives?

....

....

....

....

....

Chapter 4: A Nice Party with a Lot of People

I said in my heart, "Come now, I will test you with pleasure; enjoy yourself."
But behold, this also was vanity. (Ecclesiastes 2:1 ESV)

Vanity and feeding on the wind: that was the conclusion Solomon reached
after a life of revelry, self-indulgence, and preeminent political power.

1. Why is it so hard for us to see that this way gives no real fulfillment
   in life?

....

....

....

....

Chapter 5: Shopping for the Holy Grail

And he said to them, "Take care, and be on your guard against all covetousness, for one's life does not consist in the abundance of his possessions."
(Luke 12:15 ESV)

Advertising and pop culture tempt us with pleasure-seeking pitfalls such as covetousness.

1. What stimulates covetousness?

....

....

....

2. Why did Jesus warn us about it?

....

....

....

3. How can you respond to the warning Jesus gave?

....

....

....

Notes

HOW DO WE KNOW
WHAT'S TRUE?

Catching Up .... (10 Minutes)

Welcome back! Today, our focus for our time together is understanding truth.

- First, spend a few moments sharing worldview messages that you observed since the last session.

- Share your thoughts regarding chapters 1–5 of *The Good Life*.

- Opening Prayer: Pray that God will help you to be open to what he wants to teach you through this session.

Key Verse

Host Tip: Ask for a volunteer to read this verse aloud. If anyone has a different translation, ask him or her to read this as well to expand the group's understanding of the verse.

> *. . . you will know the truth, and the truth will set you free.*
>
> John 8:32 (ESV)

Watch the first segment of the video and take notes in the space below. Discuss the questions at the end of the segment.

Notes:

Summary

Our society has embraced an idea of "tolerance." Tolerance demands that we affirm that all views are equally valid. We have adopted a relativistic view that denies there is any fixed truth, and that whatever works for you is true for you. Ultimately, not everything can be true: if one thing is true, it excludes others as false. The Bible teaches that Jesus is the only Truth, and the biblical worldview is true and all others are false.

- American society has replaced the idea of absolute truth with relativism—the denial that there is such a thing as truth.

- Society pressures us to be "non-judgmental" and "tolerant" (that is, not to say anything that might offend someone).

- Biblical Christianity proclaims Jesus as the Truth, and thus we must believe in truth.

Discovery Questions

1. Is it possible to be tolerant and articulate truth at the same time? If so, how?

....

....

....

....

....

....

Additional Questions for Expanded Discussion

2. Where do you see people advocating the idea that truth is relative—that different people can have different truths?

3. In what situations do you find it most difficult to combat moral relativism? How might you change your approach?

Watch the second segment of the video and take notes in the space below. Discuss the questions at the end of the segment.

Notes:

Summary

There are four ways to know truth. Three of the ways were discussed in this video segment. The fourth way is revealed in the next segment.

First, the truth is in our hearts: our consciences tell us, for example, that some things are right and others are wrong (Romans 2). Second, the Bible teaches truth. Third, the created world reveals truth, even about God (Romans 1).

- The first three ways of knowing truth are:

  – Revealed Truth in the Bible

  – Nature (Romans 1)

  – Conscience (Romans 2)

- When talking with non-Christians, don't start with the Bible.

- There is ample evidence that the Bible is true.

Discovery Questions

1. Which of these three approaches to knowing truth do you think is the most effective defense of the faith? Why?

....

....

....

....

....

Additional Questions for Expanded Discussion

2. Which of these three is the most difficult to explain? Why?

3. What are some areas where relativists act as if there is truth?

Watch the third segment of the video and take notes in the space below. Discuss the questions at the end of the segment.

Notes:

Summary

The fourth way to know truth is by comparing ideas with the way the world actually works. Truth is that which conforms to reality, and only the biblical worldview can pass this test. We can use these four questions as a tool for testing the validity of competing worldviews:

1. Where did I come from?
2. Why is the world such a mess?
3. Is there a solution?
4. What is my purpose?

When a worldview provides answers to questions incorrectly, bad consequences follow.

- The fourth way of knowing truth is to compare worldviews to reality and see how well they work.

- Only the biblical worldview answers the questions correctly; every other worldview breaks down.

- Comparing worldviews is a great starting point for talking to non–Christians.

Discovery Questions

1. How can you use the four worldview questions to show people that their worldviews do not work, but that the biblical worldview does?

....

....

....

....

....

Additional Questions for Expanded Discussion

2. How would you answer someone who said there was no such thing as truth?

3. What are some good examples of biblical answers to the four worldview questions?

Living on Purpose .... (10 Minutes)

Evangelism

We live in a society that questions whether absolute truth exists, or if it does, whether it is knowable. However, in our key verse, John 8:32, Jesus promises us that we will know the truth and that this will set us free.

- What are some of the ways that people around you are enslaved by not knowing the truth?

....

....

....

....

- In what ways can you share the truth to bring the freedom of Christ to people in these situations? Will you do it? Come prepared to share any experiences you have had at the next meeting.

....

....

....

....

....

Prayer Direction .... (10 Minutes)

As you close the meeting:

- Thank God that he has made it possible for us to know the truth about the world around us, our neighbors, and ourselves. Thank him especially for the opportunity to know the truth in Jesus, who is himself, the truth.

- Ask God to help you grow in your knowledge of the truth, and ask for the wisdom and courage to share the truth with others.

Putting It into Practice

Pay attention this week to the truth claims you encounter in your daily life, from supermarket tabloids touting a "scientific discovery" (claiming that if scientists say it, it must be true), to people saying "that's true for you" (claiming truth is relative and personal).

- What attitudes toward truth are demonstrated in these truth claims?

....

....

- How would you apply the four worldview questions to test the validity of these truth claims? Come prepared to share these next week.

....

....

Diving Deeper

> *Read the following chapters of* The Good Life, *reflect on the Scripture verses listed, and answer the questions:*

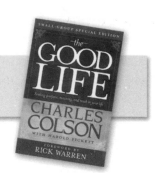

Chapter 6: Laughing at Death

[54] *When the perishable puts on the imperishable, and the mortal puts on immortality, then shall come to pass the saying that is written: "Death is swallowed up in victory."* [55] *"O death, where is your victory? O death, where is your sting?"* (1 Corinthians 15:54–55 ESV)

Death is no laughing matter for most people. Indeed, they want to avoid it at all costs.

- Laugh at death? How could anyone take such a notion seriously?

Chapter 7: More Important than Life Itself

. . . what is man that you are mindful of him, and the son of man that you care for him? (Psalm 8:4 ESV)

- If humans are not merely material/sensual beings, then is there something deeper, more enduring, or moral that drives us?

....

....

....

....

....

- Think about people you know who are more than seekers of "stuff" and sensuality? How do they demonstrate their values?

....

....

....

....

....

Chapter 8: A Life of Significance

²³Whatever you do, work heartily, as for the Lord and not for men, ²⁴knowing that from the Lord you will receive the inheritance as your reward. You are serving the Lord Christ. (Colossians 3:23–24 ESV)

- Ask some of your co-workers their reasons for going to work each day. Ask them to share what motivates them.

....

....

....

....

- What, besides earning a living, do they look to their work to provide?

....

....

....

- What do their answers reveal about them?

....

....

....

....

Chapter 9: A Silent Good-Bye

²²The rich man also died and was buried, ²³and in Hades, being in torment, he lifted up his eyes and saw Abraham far off and Lazarus at his side. ²⁴And he called out, "Father Abraham, have mercy on me . . ." (Luke 16:22–24 ESV)

"Too soon old, too late smart," so goes the old proverb. Imagine that you had known the rich man of Jesus' parable as he lay dying.

- How might you have counseled him before his last good-bye?

....

....

....

....

....

....

....

....

....

....

Chapter 10: My Happiness, Right or Wrong

¹Blessed is the man who walks not in the counsel of the wicked, nor stands in the way of sinners, nor sits in the seat of scoffers; ²but his delight is in the law of the LORD *. . .* (Psalm 1:1–2 ESV)

Our generation seems to believe it can "self-help" itself to happiness—weight loss, exercise, more sex appeal, wealth through investments, etc. But the true source of happiness—blessedness—lies elsewhere.

• Why does the psalmist's way make more sense?

WHERE DID WE COME FROM?

Catching Up .... (10 Minutes)

Welcome back! You are to be commended for your faithfulness to these sessions. Today, our major focus is to understand the origin of man.

- Reflect on what you observed regarding "truth claims" since our last meeting.

- Share your thoughts regarding chapters 6–10 of *The Good Life*.

- Opening Prayer: Pray that God will help you to be open to what he wants to teach you through this series.

Key Verse

> *Host Tip: Ask for a volunteer to read this verse aloud. If anyone has a different translation, ask him or her to read this as well to expand the group's understanding of the verse.*

Do you not know? Have you not heard?

The Lord is the everlasting God, the Creator of the ends of the earth.

Isaiah 40:28a (NIV)

Watch the first segment of the video and take notes in the space below. Discuss the questions at the end of the segment.

Notes:

Summary

God loves us and he made us for a purpose. Although we cannot contemplate life without a purpose, naturalism cannot supply us with one. According to the naturalism worldview, we are a result of random mutations and are effectively "complex slime." Despite this, naturalism, buoyed by Darwinism, is the dominant worldview in secular society today. Darwinism arose in an era that was moving away from biblical truth and replacing Christianity with enlightenment thought.

- God made us in his image, which gives each of us innate dignity and provides the essential foundation for ethics.

- The naturalist, who believes in Darwinian evolution, denies our creation and thus has no basis for human worth.

- Naturalists (evolutionists) know that they do have innate value even if they can't find a reason for it in their worldview.

Discovery Questions

1. Why is the biblical idea that we are created in the image of God so important?

....

....

....

....

....

....

Additional Questions for Expanded Discussion

2. What is the connection between Darwinism and moral relativism? How does this lead to the ethical problems we see around us today?

3. How do you think science and theology should interact today?

Watch the second segment of the video and take notes in the space below. Discuss the questions at the end of the segment.

Notes:

Summary

Darwinism is so popular because it cuts out the foundations for morality and allows us to live how we want to live. It leads to Social Darwinism, Eugenics, and other movements that deny the value of human life. But Darwinism has significant credibility weaknesses:

- *Lack of intermediate fossils*
- *Cambrian Explosion*
- *No one has successfully created a new species*
- *Presence of both altruism and homosexuality*

Each of these illustrates the weaknesses of Darwinism.

Intelligent Design is a scientific alternative based on the idea that living organisms are irreducibly complex and thus could not have evolved gradually over time. Intelligent Design's conclusions fall in line with the biblical worldview.

- There is a substantial and growing body of scientific evidence against Darwinism and for Intelligent Design.

- Darwinism is not just science, but a worldview.

- We should answer science with science, not with theory and not with Scripture, but we must also challenge the Darwinian worldview.

Discovery Questions

1. How is Darwinism more than just science?

   ....

   ....

   ....

   ....

Additional Questions for Expanded Discussion

2. What are the worldview ideas behind Darwinism?

3. Why do you think so many Christians have been involved in the sciences over the centuries?

4. What is your response to the statement, "Intelligent Design theory is religion disguised as science"?

Watch the third segment of the video and take notes in the space below. Discuss the questions at the end of the segment.

Notes:

Summary

Evolution leaves humanity without purpose. Camus states, "In the face of the meaninglessness of the universe, the only serious philosophical question is suicide." Further, it requires far more faith to be an atheist, since the evidence for a creator is overwhelming. In contrast, biblical worldview tells us that we need to find our purpose and fulfill it, giving our lives value and meaning. The biblical worldview also protects and promotes life in a way naturalism does not.

- The logical result of naturalism is nihilism—the idea that life is purposeless and nothing matters.

- The image of God gives all human life sanctity, value, meaning, and purpose.

- The biblical view of humanity and human worth is under attack today on all fronts, and we must be prepared to defend it.

Discovery Questions

1. How are "sanctity of life" issues related to the first worldview question: "Where did I come from?"

....

....

....

Additional Questions for Expanded Discussion

2. Where do you see the value of human life under attack? What are the worldview ideas behind these attacks?

3. What can we do to promote the sanctity of life in all its phases?

4. How would you explain the need for a biblical worldview in place of naturalism?

Living on Purpose .... (10 Minutes)

Worship

The wonder and beauty of nature have moved people to worship throughout the centuries.

- Identify times when you were moved by creation to worship the Creator. Share them with the group.

....

....

....

....

- Read Psalms 8, 19, and 139 and discuss what each reveals about God as our creator.

....

....

....

....

Prayer Direction .... (10 Minutes)

- In light of the Psalms you just read, spend time in worship, praising and thanking God for creation in general and his creation of humanity (and you!) in particular. Thank him for your senses and the ability to enjoy and appreciate the world, and for your mind that helps you understand it. Thank him for the meaning and purpose that our lives have because we were created in his image.

Putting It into Practice

- Watch the media for reports on origins. What worldview do you see underlying the reporting?

....

....

....

- If possible, ask teachers in your area what they are teaching about origins, both of the physical universe and of humans. Then, ask students what they know about our origins. Are the answers the same? If they are different, why do you think that is the case?

....

....

....

- Ask people you know what they think of Intelligent Design. If they think of it as religion or Creationism, share with them why Intelligent Design is actually a scientific theory.

....

....

....

....

....

....

....

....

....

....

....

....

Diving Deeper

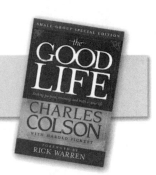

Read the following chapters of The Good Life, *reflect on the Scripture verses listed, and answer the questions.*

Chapter 11: Whose Life is It?

[18]Pride goes before destruction, and a haughty spirit before a fall. [19]It is better to be of a lowly spirit with the poor than to divide the spoil with the proud. (Proverbs 16:18–19 ESV)

Today it is almost a sacred American right to be autonomous and free to choose whatever we want. But, there are always other people to consider.

- Why is it fruitless to try to define our happiness apart from a consideration of others?

....

....

Chapter 12: A Very Rich Man

[7]Do not be deceived: God is not mocked, for whatever one sows, that will he also reap . . . [10a]So then, as we have opportunity, let us to do good to everyone . . . (Galatians 6:7, 10a ESV)

> "He is no fool who gives what he cannot keep, to gain what he cannot lose."
>
> —Jim Elliot, *Martyred Missionary*

• How does Elliot's statement echo the teaching of the Apostle Paul in our passage?

....

....

....

Chapter 13: Living Legacies

⁹*Let love be genuine. Abhor what is evil; hold fast to what is good.* ¹⁰ᵃ*Love one another with brotherly affection . . .* (Romans 12:9–10a ESV)

Social security is in a state of disarray. Corporate retirement plans are cutting back. The "golden years" of retirement do not look as promising as in the past.

• How can people start banking a "legacy of love"?

....

....

....

Chapter 14: Greater Love Hath No Man than This

¹²*"This is my commandment, that you love one another as I have loved you.* ¹³*Greater love has no one than this, that someone lays down his life for his friends."* (John 15:12–13 ESV)

- What are some of the ways, short of physical death, that we might lay down our lives for others?

....

....

- How do these kinds of actions impact others?

....

....

- What do they suggest about God's purpose for our lives?

....

....

Chapter 15: My Life for Yours—But to What End?

. . . but God shows his love for us in that while we were still sinners, Christ died for us. (Romans 5:8 ESV)

Often, our love is a fleeting affection. We love as long as the person is lovable. But Christ demonstrated true love, and died for us while we were not lovable.

- What can Christ's example teach us about love?

....

....

Notes

IT'S A MESSED UP
WORLD

Catching Up .... (10 Minutes)

Welcome back! Today, the focus for our time together is understanding the state of the world.

- Spend a few moments sharing your thoughts about the origin of man.

- Share details from your conversations on Intelligent Design. What did you learn from these conversations?

- Opening prayer: Pray that God will help you to be open to what he wants to teach you through this session.

Key Verse

⁸If we claim to be without sin, we deceive ourselves and the truth is not in us . . .
¹⁰If we claim we have not sinned, we make [God] out to be a liar,
and his word has no place in our lives.

1 John 1:8, 10 (NIV)

Watch the first segment of the video and take notes in the space below. Discuss the questions at the end of the segment.

Notes:

Summary

Evil is a part of the human condition, and we all contribute to it. Our culture has rejected the idea of sin, placing the blame for the wrong in the world everywhere except on ourselves. Although culture and our environment may influence us, they do not determine our behavior. Once we accept responsibility for our actions, sin becomes clear. Even though God created us good, original sin has bent our natures so that we desire the wrong things and act on those desires.

- The problem with the world begins with us.

- Our society encourages us to try to deny our responsibility for evil.

- Until we accept sin and our personal responsibility for it, we will never be able to understand life.

Discovery Questions

1. Explain the impact of original sin (the fall). Why is it important?

....

....

....

....

....

Additional Questions for Expanded Discussion

2. What are the different explanations of the question, "Why is the world in such a mess?"

3. How do nature, nurture, and culture influence human behavior and sin?

Watch the second segment of the video and take notes in the space below. Discuss the questions at the end of the segment.

Notes:

Summary

The biblical worldview teaches that sin entered the world because of our free will. God made us in his image, to love him and to have a relationship with him. However, love must be freely given if it is to be real, and so God gave us the ability to reject him. Man chose the non-good rather than the good, and as a result our lives have been broken on all levels. Every sin calls into doubt God's knowledge of what is best; but, because God does know what is best, sin also hurts us and the world we live in.

- God gave us free will so we could love him. Love that isn't freely given isn't love.

- We often use our free will to reject the good which God offers us.

- All sin is based on lies, questioning whether God really loves us or knows what's best for us.

Discovery Questions

1. How do you think love, free will, and human responsibility fit together in God's plan?

....

....

....

....

....

Additional Questions for Expanded Discussion

2. Think about some of the movies, television shows, and other media you've seen recently. How do their worldviews address the problems of sin, suffering, and moral decay?

3. Where does temptation end and sin begin?

Watch the third segment of the video and take notes in the space below. Discuss the questions at the end of the segment.

Notes:

Summary

No other worldview of sin fits reality. Only the power of Christ can change us and put us on the road to living a good life. Therefore, those without Christ cannot consistently do good. We are called to recognize and identify sin without being judgmental. We need to take responsibility for our own failings and accept people without approving of their wrong choices.

- No other worldview has an adequate explanation for the evil in the world.

- Without God, people can do good things but they cannot be good.

- Recognizing sin isn't being judgmental: we can accept people without approving what they do.

- God redeems sin and suffering.

Discovery Questions

1. Compare the biblical worldview to other explanations of the problem of suffering. Which explanation makes more sense?

....

....

....

....

....

Additional Questions for Expanded Discussion

2. How have you seen God bringing good out of suffering?

3. Do you think the idea that people cannot lead a righteous life without God is harsh or judgmental? Why?

4. How do you respond when someone says, "Judge not lest ye be judged?"

Living on Purpose .... (10 Minutes)

Worship and Evangelism

When we look at the world around us, it is easy to see sin promoted in our society and the broken lives it has caused. Yet as the verses quoted at the beginning of this session remind us, sin is not limited to those "out there," but it affects each one of us. It may seem strange to discuss worship in the context of sin, yet confession has been part of worship since the Old Testament.

- Read Nehemiah 1:5–11 and Daniel 9:4–19. Neither Nehemiah nor Daniel was part of the generation that sinned, yet they still confessed personally the sins of their people. What can we learn from them in our prayers for our church, community, and country?

....

....

- 1 John 1:9 reminds us that personal confession of sin to God leads to forgiveness. Is this something you practice? How often?

....

....

- Ask God to help you have his heart for the lost around you, recognizing and mourning for sin and its effects, and building in you a zeal to share the Gospel with people who need to experience God's grace and healing.

Prayer Direction .... (10 Minutes)

- Spend some time in prayers of confession of personal and corporate sins. Thank God for the promise of forgiveness.

- Pray for people who you know are suffering. Ask God to use you to bring them hope and relief.

Putting It into Practice

One thing we hope to learn by studying differing worldviews is how they can shape people's actions and attitudes. As you go through the week, you will undoubtedly run into examples of sin and its effects in the world around you. Take some time to think about the stated or implied worldview behind the choices that produce the sin:

- What does the worldview say about the value of people?

....

....

....

....

- How does the worldview fit with reality? Come prepared to share your insights with the group at our next meeting.

Diving Deeper

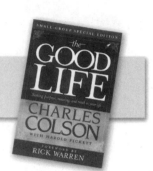

Read the following chapters of The Good Life, reflect on the Scripture verses listed, and answer the questions:

Chapter 16: Journey Into Illusion

¹⁴For when Gentiles, who do not have the law, by nature do what the law requires, they are a law to themselves, even though they do not have the law. ¹⁵They show that the work of the law is written on their hearts . . . (Romans 2:14–15 ESV)

- Do people have a built-in moral sense?

....

....

- Where does it come from?

....

- How is it expressed in our lives?

....

- What does it suggest about our nature and our purpose?

....

....

Chapter 17: Living Within the Truth

The sum of your word is truth, and every one of your righteous rules endures forever. (Psalm 119:160 ESV)

Today's generation views truth as a personal decision. But what happens to truth when everyone is free to personalize it? And how do people show that they really need some fixed truth? Where shall we find such truth?

....

....

Chapter 18: Can We Know the Truth?

Lead me in your truth and teach me, for you are the God of my salvation; for you I wait all the day long. (Psalm 25:5 ESV)

Our age is filled with "truth-schizophrenics," who deny any absolute truth then swear they are absolutely right. God says otherwise, and longs to lead us in his truth.

* How does he do that?

....

....

* What does it mean to "wait" for him in this process?

....

....

Chapter 19: What Is Life Worth?

See now that I, even I, am he, and there is no god beside me; I kill and I make alive; I wound and I heal; and there is none that can deliver out of my hand. (Deuteronomy 32:39 ESV)

People today want to "play God" when it comes to matters of life and death.

- Who decides who gets to "play"?

....

....

....

....

....

- How does this "playing God" deny the principle of loving our neighbors as we love ourselves?

....

....

....

....

....

Chapter 20: God's ID

¹Lord, you have been our dwelling place in all generations. ²Before the mountains were brought forth, or ever you had formed the earth and the world, from everlasting to everlasting you are God. (Psalm 90:1–2 ESV)

- Why is it difficult for many people to acknowledge divine evidence in the world around them?

....

....

....

- Are there moral implications to such an acknowledgment?

....

....

....

- What do they miss by denying the existence of the eternal God?

....

....

....

Notes

WHAT'S THE
SOLUTION?

Catching Up .... (10 Minutes)

Welcome back! In our last session, we asked why the world is so messed up. Today, we'll focus on redemption, reconciliation, and hope.

- What were some of the effects of sin you identified during the week? What are the worldviews associated with these sins?

- How well do these worldviews align with truth?

- Opening Prayer: Pray that God will help you to be open to what he wants to teach you about the biblical worldview.

Key Verse

⁸For by grace you have been saved through faith.
⁹And this is not your own doing; it is the gift of God,
not a result of works, so that no one may boast.

Ephesians 2:8–9 (ESV)

Watch the first segment of the video and take notes in the space below. Discuss the questions at the end of the segment.

Notes:

....

....

....

....

....

....

....

....

....

....

....

....

Summary

The world is looking for salvation in all the wrong places. Some look for it in political power and the law. Others believe education will solve all human problems. For others, the solution is found in economics and material prosperity. Still others believe that psychology will provide liberation. But none of these supposed solutions address the underlying condition of human sinfulness.

- Politics cannot solve the problems the world is facing.

- Education has not changed things much either.

- Money cannot bring ultimate satisfaction, purpose, or meaning.

- Psychology does not provide the answer.

Discovery Questions

1. What alternative "solutions" do you most often encounter? How do they affect you? How do you respond to them?

....

....

....

....

Additional Questions for Expanded Discussion

2. Have you ever been persuaded by any false offers of salvation?

3. Why do you think people resist the truth and seek other alternatives?

Watch the second segment of the video and take notes in the space below. Discuss the questions at the end of the segment.

Notes:

Summary

The universal problem we all face is guilt. We know we have sinned, and that is why we search for answers. We are not made to carry guilt. We need to surrender our lives to God so that we may be changed. We need grace; something no other religion can offer. Only Christianity, empowered by God's grace, has a worldview that results in transformed lives.

- The basic problem people have to address is guilt.

- The only solution is found in surrendering our will to God, which liberates us from all the things holding us down.

- Jesus provided redemption to us through the cross, giving us grace (an undeserved gift) so that we can be set free.

Discovery Questions

1. To be free you must first surrender your life. Why is this paradox important?

....

....

....

Additional Questions for Expanded Discussion

2. How do other worldviews handle the problem of guilt? What hope do they offer for the future?

3. What hope would you offer someone for the guilt they may be carrying?

"How to Become a Follower of Jesus Christ"

Have you ever surrendered your life to Jesus Christ? Take a few minutes with your group to watch a brief video by Pastor Rick Warren on how to become part of the family of God. It is included on the Session Five menu of this DVD.

Watch the third segment of the video and take notes in the space below. Discuss the questions at the end of the segment.

Notes:

Summary

Redemption brings reconciliation with God and with our neighbor. Reconciliation enables us to build Christian community—the church of Jesus Christ. As his church, God calls us to be agents of reconciliation to the world, sharing the gospel through our words and our actions. Over time, the gospel transforms us as we live out our faith.

- Redemption leads to reconciliation not just with God, but in all our relationships.

- Christians obey God out of gratitude for what he's done for us, not out of obligation.

- All our problems didn't go away when we became a Christian, but through grace, we can accept God's will.

Discovery Questions

1. How have you seen God's reconciling power in your life?

....

....

....

....

....

....

Additional Questions for Expanded Discussion

2. Are you facing a difficult situation in which you need to see God's grace?

3. In what practical ways can your group demonstrate Christ's redemption and reconciliation to others?

Living on Purpose .... (10 Minutes)

Fellowship

Because we have been reconciled to God through Christ, God is now our Father, we are his children, other believers are our brothers and sisters, and the church is our spiritual family.

- How should this truth shape our attitude toward fellowship?

....

....

....

....

- Have you ever been in a situation where you developed friendships with people solely because you shared a relationship with Jesus? Briefly describe the situation.

....

....

....

....

Prayer Direction .... (10 Minutes)

- Thank God for the gift of salvation.

- Thank God that in Christ we have the answers for all our needs, our relationships with others, and even answers to the broader issue of our relationship to the world around us.

- Ask God for wisdom and courage to act as agents of reconciliation wherever you are. Pray specifically for those people in need of the gospel whom God has placed in your life.

Putting It into Practice

Over the past few weeks, we have been looking at how worldviews shape the actions and attitudes of people. This week, initiate at least one conversation about worldview with someone who is not involved in this study. Seek to understand the implications of their position.

Hints:

1. Listen intently. Think about the worldview implications.

2. Ask them questions about their comments.

3. Listen carefully to their answers. If needed, ask for clarification.

4. Don't become defensive. Share your thoughts with gentleness and respect. See 1 Peter 3:15.

5. Come prepared to talk about your experience at the next session.

Diving Deeper

> Read the following chapters of The Good Life, reflect on
> the Scripture verses listed, and answer the questions:

Chapter 21: Morality and the Natural Order

⁶And because you are sons, God has sent the Spirit of his Son into your
hearts, crying, "Abba! Father!" ⁷So you are no longer a slave, but a son,
and if a son, then an heir through God. (Galatians 4:6–7 ESV)

- What kinds of things do you think enslave those who have not found
  freedom in Christ?

  ....

  ....

- How do you think this "slavery" affects them?

  ....

  ....

- How might you help a friend see this type of enslavement?

  ....

  ....

  ....

Chapter 22: The Gift of Knowing Right from Wrong

³¹So Jesus said to the Jews who had believed in him, "If you abide in my word, you are truly my disciples, ³²and you will know the truth, and the truth will set you free." (John 8:31–32 ESV)

This verse contains a formula for freedom:

> BELIEF IN HIM + ABIDING IN HIS WORD = FREEDOM

- Free from what?

  ....

  ....

  ....

- As a believer, free to what?

  ....

  ....

  ....

- How can only "true disciples" of Christ be truly free?

  ....

  ....

  ....

Chapter 23: Beauty: The Sign of God's Care

One thing I have asked of the LORD, that will I seek after: that I may dwell in the house of the LORD all the days of my life, to gaze upon the beauty of the LORD . . . (Psalm 27:4 ESV)

The world says, "Beauty is in the eye of the beholder;" but Scripture teaches that the Creator defines beauty, who is himself, beautiful.

• What evidence points to God's beauty?

....

....

....

Chapter 24: Written On the Heart

For although they knew God, they did not honor him as God or give thanks to him, but they became futile in their thinking . . . (Romans 1:21 ESV)

People take so much for granted—from a beautiful sunset to a friend's smile. Often this leads to thoughts such as, "If everything is merely the product of time, chance, and matter, why should we be thankful?"

• Where does such thanklessness lead?

....

....

• How might you cultivate a life of thanksgiving?

....

....

....

....

....

Chapter 25: Postmodernists in Recovery

There is a way that seems right to a man, but its end is the way to death.
(Proverbs 14:12 ESV)

Postmodernism has boiled truth down to the dregs of sentimentality and individualism. Yet many are looking for something more substantial.

• Imagine a conversation with a postmodernist. What questions would help that person consider a biblical view of truth?

....

....

....

....

....

Notes

WHAT DO I DO
NOW?

Catching Up .... (10 Minutes)

Welcome back! Today, we'll focus on our ministry and mission.

- Did you have a conversation this week with someone whose worldview differs from yours? Share your experience with the group.

- Opening Prayer: Pray that God will help you be open to what he wants to teach you through this session.

Key Verse

And whatever you do, in word or deed,
do everything in the name of the Lord Jesus,
giving thanks to God the Father through him.

Colossians 3:17 (ESV)

Watch the first segment of the video and take notes in the space below. Discuss the questions at the end of the segment.

Notes:

Summary

God has given us two commissions: the Great Commission, to make disciples, and the Cultural Commission, to act as God's representatives in protecting and developing the world he created. The Cultural Commission is part of the Great Commandment, to love God with all our heart, soul, mind, and strength. Our vocation, whatever it may be, is a calling from God to live out our worldview and to bring his rule to bear in our workplace.

- Christians have two commissions, the Great Commission, to make disciples, and the Cultural Commission, to protect and develop God's creation.

- Your vocation is an area of ministry for you, whatever it is.

Discovery Questions

1. In what ways could you see your work as an area of ministry?

....

....

....

....

....

....

Additional Questions for Expanded Discussion

2. How do you view work? Is it a good thing or a bad thing?

3. Which commission takes pre-eminence in your life? How can we balance them effectively?

Watch the second segment of the video and take notes in the space below. Discuss the questions at the end of the segment.

Notes:

Summary

The biblical worldview says that God's sovereignty influences every area of life. It provides the foundations for economic development and justice. Our concepts of freedom, the rule of law, and limited government come from the Bible. Most early leaders of modern science were Christians; and only the biblical worldview provides a solid foundation for science. The arts too are founded in Scripture and are a reflection of God's beauty and his will for creation.

- Business and economics, law and government, and science have all developed through Christianity's influence on culture.

- The biblical worldview holds that art should reflect objective standards of beauty rooted in God.

- Christianity has important things to say about how we work in each area of life.

Discovery Questions

1. In what area of your life do you have the most difficulty recognizing God's sovereignty?

   ....

   ....

   ....

   ....

   ....

Additional Questions for Expanded Discussion

2. Where in your sphere of influence is the biblical worldview most desperately needed?

3. What new ideas have you gained about how to carry out the Cultural Commission in your work and in your daily life?

Watch the third segment of the video and take notes in the space below. Discuss the questions at the end of the segment.

Notes:

Summary

As we seek to apply the biblical worldview to all of life, we must not try to impose it on others; instead, we should propose a better way of life to them. We must approach our task with humility, humor and grace, always seeking to persuade, not coerce. We should honor those who oppose us, recognizing in them the image of God, as we live out the love of God in all our relationships. We change lives first, then culture, as we work to overcome evil with good.

- We do not want to impose our views on others; instead, we want to propose something better.

- Keep learning about worldviews.

- Lovingly challenge people about their worldviews, and introduce them to something better.

- Overcome evil with good.

Discovery Questions

1. What do you find most challenging about living out the biblical worldview?

....

....

....

....

....

Additional Questions for Expanded Discussion

2. What concrete steps are you going to take to bring a biblical worldview into every facet of your life?

3. What areas of culture are you passionate about? What steps can you take to impact culture with a Christian worldview?

4. Read 1 Peter 3:15. How can we propose a biblical worldview without imposing it on others?

Living on Purpose .... (10 Minutes)

Ministry and Mission

The fourth worldview question, "What is my purpose?" is all about what we do with the answers to the first three questions. To the Christian, this means our calling to love God and love our neighbor "not in word or talk but in deed and in truth" (1 John 3:18, ESV). We live out this calling through our ministry in the church and through our mission in the world: a mission that includes not simply evangelism to fulfill the Great Commission, but stewardship to fulfill the Cultural Commission.

1. What is your calling? How can you fulfill the Cultural Commission in each of the following areas:

   • Family

   • Business

- Community

- Personal Growth

- Recreation

2. In what ways are you using the gifts God has given you in service to his church? Is there any ministry that you feel called to that you are not currently pursuing? What can you do to begin?

Prayer Direction .... (10 Minutes)

- Thank God for what you have learned in this study.

- Ask God for grace and courage to share the biblical worldview with others.

Putting It into Practice

God has called you to advance his kingdom in all areas of life, acting as his steward and ambassador to the world around you. The first step to fulfilling this call is to renew your commitment to reading the Bible and developing a deeper understanding of the biblical worldview.

Next, develop the habit of analyzing movies, television shows, newspapers, and even the comments of people around you, to understand their worldviews. Then, "with gentleness and respect," propose a better way; showing people through your words and your life how things are meant to be.

Diving Deeper

Read the following chapters of The Good Life, *reflect on the Scripture verses listed, and answer the questions:*

Chapter 26: Hope, Freedom, and Happiness

"For I know the plans I have for you," declares the LORD, *"plans for wholeness and not for evil, to give you a future and a hope."* (Jeremiah 29:11 ESV)

Are you a "hope-giver?" God gives joy and hope to those who trust him and participate in his kingdom work.

- How does he give us hope?

....

....

....

....

- What can we learn from him about being "hope-givers" to one another?

....

....

....

Chapter 27: The Bad News

¹⁵. . . For I do not do what I want, but I do the very thing I hate . . . ¹⁷So now it is no longer I who do it, but sin that dwells within me. (Romans 7:15, 17 ESV)

Have you ever had one of those days when, despite all your efforts, you end up doing the wrong thing? There is a war going on within us.

- How can we encourage one another in this struggle against indwelling sin?

Chapter 28: Providence

And we know that for those who love God all things work together for good, for those who are called according to his purpose. (Romans 8:28 ESV)

Too often, we lose sight of God's providence. The chaos of everyday life can sometimes leave us feeling out of control.

- How would you counsel someone to hold onto the truth of Romans 8:28 in the midst of some trial or disappointment?

Chapter 29: A Good Death

For to me to live is Christ, and to die is gain. (Philippians 1:21 ESV)

Augustine wrote, "A bad death never follows a good life: for there is nothing that maketh death bad but that estate which followeth death" (City of God, I.x).

- Do you believe this is true? Why or why not?

....

....

....

- Can we know what the "estate which followeth death" will be for us? How?

....

....

....

- How can we encourage one another with this news?

....

....

....

....

Chapter 30: Infinite Truth and Love

⁵Thomas said to him, "Lord, we do not know where you are going. How can we know the way?" ⁶Jesus said to him, "I am the way, and the truth, and the life. No one comes to the Father except through me." (John 14:5–6 ESV)

The postmodernist says, "Any way that suits you will do. Truth is what you make it. It's my life and I'll do what I want."

• How would Jesus answer those claims?

....

....

....

....

• How can you answer those claims?

....

....

....

....

Notes

GROUP
RESOURCES

Helps for Hosts

Top Ten Ideas for New Hosts

Congratulations! As the host of your small group, you have responded to the call to help shepherd Jesus' flock. Few other tasks in the family of God surpass the contribution you will be making. As you prepare to facilitate your group, whether it is one session or the entire series, here are a few thoughts to keep in mind.

Remember you are not alone. God knows everything about you, and he knew you would be asked to facilitate your group. Even though you may not feel ready, this is common for all good hosts. God promises, *"I will never leave you; I will never abandon you"* (Hebrews 13:5 TEV). Whether you are facilitating for one evening, several weeks, or a lifetime, you will be blessed as you serve.

1. **Don't try to do it alone.** Pray right now for God to help you build a healthy team. If you can enlist a co-host to help you shepherd the group, you will find your experience much richer. This is your chance to involve as many people as you can in building a healthy group. All you have to do is ask people to help. You'll be surprised at the response.

2. **Be friendly and be yourself.** God wants to use your unique gifts and temperament. Be sure to greet people at the door with a big smile. This can set the mood for the whole gathering. Remember, they are taking as big a step show up at your house as you are to host this group! Don't try to do things exactly like another host; do them in a way that fits you. Admit when you don't have an answer and apologize when you make a mistake. Your group will love you for it and you'll sleep better at night.

3. **Prepare for your meeting ahead of time.** Review the session and write down your responses to each question. Pay special attention to exercises that ask group members to do something other than engage in discussion. These exercises will help your group live what the Bible teaches, not just talk about it. Be sure you understand how an exercise works. If the exercise employs one of the items in the Group Resources section (such as the Group Guidelines), be sure to look over that item so you'll know how it works.

4. **Pray for your group members by name.** Before you begin your session, take a few moments and pray for each member by name. You may want to review the prayer list at least once a week. Ask God to use your time together to touch the heart of every person in your group. Expect God to lead you to whomever he wants you to encourage or challenge in a special way. If you listen, God will surely lead.

5. **When you ask a question, be patient.** Someone will eventually respond. Sometimes people need a moment or two of silence to think about the question. If silence doesn't bother you, it won't bother anyone else. After someone responds, affirm the response with a simple "thanks" or "great answer." Then ask, "How about somebody else?" or "Would someone who hasn't shared like to add anything?" Be sensitive to new people or reluctant members who aren't ready to say, pray, or do anything. If you give them a safe setting, they will blossom over time. If someone in your group is a "wall flower" who sits silently through every session, consider talking to them privately and encouraging them to participate. Let them know how important they are to you—that they are loved and appreciated, and that the group would value their input. Remember, still water often runs deep.

6. **Provide transitions between questions.** Ask if anyone would like to read the paragraph or Bible passage. Don't call on anyone, but ask for a volunteer, and then be patient until someone begins. Be sure to thank the person who reads aloud.

7. **Break into smaller groups occasionally.** With a greater opportunity to talk in a small circle, people will connect more with the study, apply more quickly what they're learning, and ultimately get more out of their small group experience. A small circle also encourages a quiet person to participate and tends to minimize the effects of a more vocal or dominant member.

8. **Small circles are also helpful during prayer time.** People who are unaccustomed to praying aloud will feel more comfortable trying it with just two or three others. Also, prayer requests won't take as much time, so circles will have more time to actually pray. When you gather back with the whole group, you can have one person from each circle briefly update everyone on the prayer requests from their subgroups. The other great aspect of subgrouping is that it fosters leadership development. As you ask people in the group to facilitate discussion or to lead a prayer circle, it gives them a small leadership step that can build their confidence.

9. **Rotate facilitators occasionally.** You may be perfectly capable of hosting each time, but you will help others grow in their faith and gifts if you give them opportunities to host the group.

10. **One final challenge (for new or first-time hosts).** Before your first opportunity to lead, look up each of the five passages listed below. Read each one as a devotional exercise to help prepare you with a shepherd's heart. Trust us on this one. If you do this, you will be more than ready for your first meeting.

Matthew 9:36–38 (NIV)

36When Jesus saw the crowds, he had compassion on them, because they were harassed and helpless, like sheep without a shepherd. 37Then he said to his disciples, "The harvest is plentiful but the workers are few. 38Ask the Lord of the harvest, therefore, to send out workers into his harvest field."

John 10:14–15 (NIV)

14I am the good shepherd; I know my sheep and my sheep know me—15just as the Father knows me and I know the Father—and I lay down my life for the sheep.

1 Peter 5:2–4 (NIV)

²Be shepherds of God's flock that is under your care, serving as overseers—not because you must, but because you are willing, as God wants you to be; ³not greedy for money, but eager to serve; not lording it over those entrusted to you, but being examples to the flock. ⁴And when the Chief Shepherd appears, you will receive the crown of glory that will never fade away.

Philippians 2:1–5 (NIV)

¹If you have any encouragement from being united with Christ, if any comfort from his love, if any fellowship with the Spirit, if any tenderness and compassion, ²then make my joy complete by being like-minded, having the same love, being one in spirit and purpose. ³Do nothing out of selfish ambition or vain conceit, but in humility consider others better than yourselves. ⁴Each of you should look not only to your own interests, but also to the interests of others. ⁵Your attitude should be the same as that of Jesus Christ.

Hebrews 10:23–25 (NIV)

²³Let us hold unswervingly to the hope we profess, for he who promised is faithful. ²⁴And let us consider how we may spur one another on toward love and good deeds. ²⁵Let us not give up meeting together, as some are in the habit of doing, but let us encourage one another—and all the more as you see the Day approaching.

1 Thessalonians 2:7–8, 11–12 (NIV)

⁷. . . but we were gentle among you, like a mother caring for her little children. ⁸We loved you so much that we were delighted to share with you not only the Gospel of God but our lives as well, because you had become so dear to us. . . . ¹¹For you know that we dealt with each of you as a father deals with his own children, ¹²encouraging, comforting and urging you to live lives worthy of God, who calls you into his kingdom and glory.

Frequently Asked Questions

How long will this group meet?

Wide Angle: Framing Your Worldview is six sessions long. We encourage your group to add a seventh session for a celebration. In your final session, each group member may decide if he or she desires to continue on for another study. At that time you may also want to do some informal evaluation, discuss your group guidelines, and decide which study you want to do next. We recommend you visit our website at **www.purposedriven.com** for more video-based small group studies.

Who is the host?

The host is the person who coordinates and facilitates your group meetings. In addition to a host, we encourage you to select one or more group members to lead your group discussions. Several other responsibilities can be rotated, including refreshments, prayer requests, worship, or keeping up with those who miss a meeting. Shared ownership in the group helps everybody grow.

Where do we find new group members?

Recruiting new members can be a challenge for groups, especially new groups with just a few people, or existing groups that lose a few people along the way. We encourage you to use the Circles of Life diagram on page 126 of this workbook to brainstorm a list of people from your workplace, church, school, neighborhood, family, and so on. Then pray for the people on each member's list. Allow each member to invite several people from their list.

Some groups fear that newcomers will interrupt the intimacy that members have built over time. However, groups that welcome newcomers generally gain strength with the infusion of new blood. Remember, the next person you add just might become a friend for eternity. Logistically, groups find different ways to add members. Some groups remain permanently open, while others choose to open periodically, such as at the beginning or end of a study. If your group becomes too large for easy, face-to-face conversations, you can subgroup, forming a second discussion group in another room.

How do we handle the childcare needs in our group?

Childcare needs must be handled very carefully. This is a sensitive issue. We suggest you seek creative solutions as a group. One common solution is to have the adults meet in the living room and share the cost of a baby sitter (or two) who can be with the kids in another part of the house. Another popular option is to have one home for the kids and a second home (close by) for the adults. If desired, the adults could rotate the responsibility of providing a lesson for the kids. This last option is great with school age kids and can be a huge blessing to families.

Group Guidelines

It's a good idea for every group to put words to their shared values, expectations, and commitments. Such guidelines will help you avoid unspoken agendas and unmet expectations. We recommend you discuss your guidelines during Session One in order to lay the foundation for a healthy group experience. Feel free to modify anything that does not work for your group.

We agree to the following values:

Clear Purpose   To grow healthy spiritual lives by building a healthy small group community

Group Attendance   To give priority to the group meeting (call if I am absent or late)

Safe Environment   To create a safe place where people can be heard and feel loved (no quick answers, snap judgments, or simple fixes)

Be Confidential   To keep anything that is shared strictly confidential and within the group

Conflict Resolution   To avoid gossip and to immediately resolve any concerns by following the principles of Matthew 18:15–17

Spiritual Health   To give group members permission to speak into my life and help me live a healthy, balanced spiritual life that is pleasing to God

Limit Our Freedom   To limit our freedom by not serving or consuming alcohol during small group meetings or events so as to avoid causing a weaker brother or sister to stumble (1 Corinthians 8:1–13; Romans 14:19–21)

Welcome Newcomers   To invite friends who might benefit from this study and warmly welcome newcomers

Building Relationships To get to know the other members of the group and pray for them regularly

Other _____

_____

We have also discussed and agree on the following items:

Child Care _____

_____

Starting Time _____

Ending Time _____

If you haven't already done so, take a few minutes to fill out the Small Group Calendar on page 131.

Circles of Life: Small Group Connections

Discover Who You Can Connect in Community

Use this chart to help carry out one of the values in the Group Guidelines, to "Welcome Newcomers."

"Follow me, and I will make you fishers of men." (Matthew 4:19 KJV)

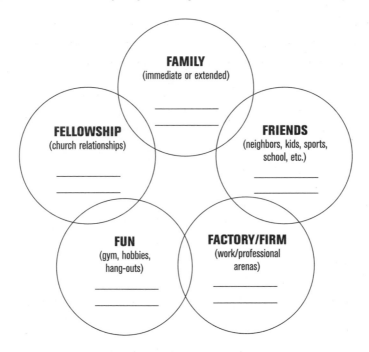

Follow this simple three-step process:

1. List one to two people in each circle.

2. Prayerfully select one person or couple from your list and tell your group about them.

3. Give them a call and invite them to your next meeting. Over fifty percent of those invited to a small group say, "Yes!"

Small Group Prayer and Praise Report

This is a place where you can write each other's requests for prayer. You can also make a note when God answers a prayer. Pray for each other's requests. If you're new to group prayer, it's okay to pray silently or to pray by using just one sentence:

"God, please help _____ to _____ ."

DATE	PERSON	PRAYER REQUEST	PRAISE REPORT

Small Group Prayer and Praise Report

DATE	PERSON	PRAYER REQUEST	PRAISE REPORT

Small Group Prayer and Praise Report

DATE	PERSON	PRAYER REQUEST	PRAISE REPORT

Small Group Prayer and Praise Report

DATE	PERSON	PRAYER REQUEST	PRAISE REPORT

Small Group Calendar

Healthy groups share responsibilities and group ownership. It might take some time for this to develop. Shared ownership ensures that responsibility for the group doesn't fall to one person. Use the calendar to keep track of social events, mission projects, birthdays, or days off. Complete this calendar at your first or second meeting. Planning ahead will increase attendance and shared ownership.

DATE	LESSON	LOCATION	FACILITATOR	SNACK OR MEAL
10/22	Session 2	Steve and Laura	Bill Jones	John and Alice

Charles Colson is perhaps best-known today as an evangelical leader whose insightful commentary on cultural trends from a biblical perspective has shaped the landscape of Christian thought. But over thirty years ago, he was better known as President Nixon's hatchet man and as a figure in the Watergate scandal.

When news of Colson's conversion to Christianity leaked to the press in 1973, the Boston Globe reported, "If Mr. Colson can repent of his sins, there just has to be hope for everybody." Colson would agree. For his role in Watergate, Colson spent seven months in a federal prison.

In 1976, Colson founded Prison Fellowship, the world's largest outreach to prisoners, ex-prisoners, and their families. He has become a leading author and commentator, having written more than twenty books, which have collectively sold more than five million copies. In 1999, Colson and Nancy Pearcey co-authored the groundbreaking book *How Now Shall We Live?* challenging Christians to understand biblical faith as an entire worldview, a perspective on all of life.

His daily radio program, "BreakPoint," which airs on more than 1,000 radio outlets, provides a distinct Christian worldview on today's critical issues and trends.

Prison Fellowship

Prison Fellowship (PF) encompasses two ministries:

- Prison Fellowship, which seeks the transformation of prisoners and their reconciliation to God, family and community through the power and truth of Jesus Christ; and

- BreakPoint, the transformation of believers as they apply biblical thinking to all of life, enabling them to transform their communities through the grace and truth of Jesus Christ.

Prison Fellowship partners with churches across the United States to strike at the very heart of crime—by offering prisoners the hope and transforming power of Jesus Christ. Founded by Chuck Colson in 1976, Prison Fellowship is now active in every state of the U.S. and in 111 other countries around the world.

Prison Fellowship reaches out to prisoners through a variety of seminars, Bible studies, mentoring programs, and special events; and continues to minister to them after their release through church-based aftercare programs. In addition, Prison Fellowship's Angel Tree® program unites thousands of churches in reaching out to the children of prisoners at Christmas and throughout the year, helping to reconcile families and transform lives through the power of Jesus Christ.

BreakPoint, our worldview teaching ministry, equips believers to think about all of life from a biblical perspective and to speak biblical truth persuasively to a culture in crisis. BreakPoint employs a variety of venues to defend and teach biblical worldview—radio broadcasts, curricula development, interactive online commentaries, an intensive distance-learning program, and both print and online publications. BreakPoint also exerts a significant influence in the area of legislation and public policy development, impacting such critical issues as stem cell research and experimentation, marriage and family values, human-rights abuses, and more.

www.pfm.org
www.breakpoint.org
1-877-478-0100

How Now Shall We Live?

This book is a stimulating challenge to all believers to be prepared to effectively evangelize, and to lay bare the truth about our society's false beliefs. Chuck Colson shares a comprehensive perspective for Christian living and faith building, and how to apply a biblical eye to the issues in the world around us. You can order online at *www.breakpoint.org*.

Item Code: BKHNS
Suggested Donation: $25

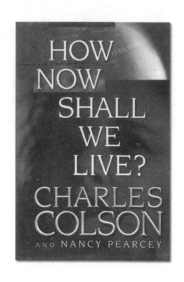

Rewired: A Teen Worldview Curriculum

Rewired was co-produced by Chuck Colson and the cutting-edge youth ministry Teen Mania. This DVD-based, visually rich curriculum tackles the key worldview questions and explores how those answers can impact teens' ideas, beliefs, and attitudes—concerning everything from life-or-death issues such as abortion and doctor-assisted suicide, to everyday dilemmas of what kind of outfit to wear to school or what music to download.

Your youth will learn to expose prevalent false ideas promoted in our culture. They'll discover the Christian perspective on the issues and find ways to counter distorted ideas with confidence and clarity. You can order online at *www.breakpoint.org/rewired*, or call 1-877-3-CALLBP.

Item Code: Rewired-KT
Suggested Donation $80

Answers to Your Kids' Questions

This informative book by Chuck Colson offers up answers to 100 important questions that teens are asking about God, science, morality, and other worldview issues. A companion volume to *How Now Shall We Live?*, the book provides a great way to open up a dialog with the young people in your life. You can order online at *www.breakpoint.org.*

Item Code: BKAKQ
Suggested Donation: $20

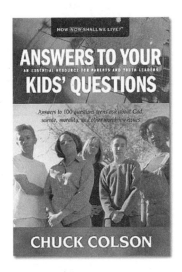

BreakPoint WorldView Magazine

BreakPoint WorldView magazine includes articles on popular culture, the arts, natural law, public policy issues—and more—offering a "Christian perspective on today's news and trends." It also includes editorials, updates from Capitol Hill, and the best of BreakPoint® radio commentaries by Chuck Colson. For a donation of $25 or more, you will receive a one-year subscription (ten issues). It makes a great gift for friends, family, and college students you may know. You can order online at *www.breakpoint.org*, or call 1-800-995-8777.

Suggested Donation: $25

S.H.A.P.E.

Find & Fulfill Your Unique Purpose for Life

In his book, *The Purpose Driven® Life*, Rick Warren introduced the concept of S.H.A.P.E.—Spiritual gifts, Heart, Abilities, Personality, Experiences—and showed us how God uses each of our unique S.H.A.P.E.s to release us into ministry.

In this video-based small group study, Erik Rees builds on Rick Warren's foundational teaching by taking you through the process of discovering your own deeply personal S.H.A.P.E.—the remarkable elements that work together to make you who you are, and that point you to the life-purpose God has planned just for you.

Discover God's most powerful and effective means of advancing his kingdom: You! Learn how God can use your own irreplaceable, richly detailed, personal S.H.A.P.E., empowered by the Holy Spirit, to accomplish his purposes on the earth!

- Unlock your God-given potential!
- Uncover your specific kingdom purpose!
- Unfold a kingdom plan for your life!

You are uniquely S.H.A.P.E.d to bring glory to God. Find out how, through this life-changing small group study.

Available now at *www.purposedriven.com*.

40 Days of Purpose

Small Group Edition

Based on the best-selling book, *The Purpose Driven® Life* by Rick Warren, this curriculum is uniquely designed for church members and new believers who desire to fulfill God's purpose for their lives.

40 Days of Purpose Small Group Edition is also great for those who want to review the material in their new or existing small group/class, share it with a friend, or even for pastors who want to review the five purposes with their church family.

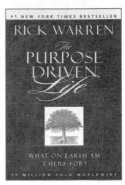

The Way of a Worshiper

The pursuit of God is the chase of a lifetime—in fact, it's been going on since the day you were born. The question is: Have you been the hunter or the prey?

This small group study is not about music. It's not even about going to church. It's about living your life as an offering of worship to God. It's about tapping into the source of power to live the Christian life. And it's about discovering the secret to friendship with God.

In these four video sessions, Buddy Owens helps you unpack the meaning of worship. Through his very practical, engaging, and at times surprising insights, Buddy shares truths from Scripture and from life that will help you understand in a new and deeper way just what it means to be a worshiper.

God is looking for worshipers. His invitation to friendship is open and genuine. Will you take him up on his offer? Will you give yourself to him in worship? Then come walk the Way of a Worshiper and discover the secret to friendship with God.

THE WAY *of a* WORSHIPER

Your study of this material will be greatly enhanced by reading the book, *The Way of a Worshiper: Discover the Secret to Friendship with God.*